THE KOREAN AMERICANS

Brian Lehrer

CHELSEA HOUSE PUBLISHERS

New York   Philadelphia

Cover Photograph: Korean American family at their suburban home.

Editor-in-Chief: Nancy Toff
Executive Editor: Remmel T. Nunn
Managing Editor: Karyn Gullen Browne
Copy Chief: Juliann Barbato
Picture Editor: Adrian G. Allen
Art Director: Giannella Garrett
Manufacturing Manager: Gerald Levine

Staff for THE KOREAN AMERICANS:
Senior Editor: Sam Tanenhaus
Assistant Editor: Abigail Meisel
Copyeditors: Michael Goodman, James Guiry
Editorial Assistant: Theodore Keyes
Picture Researcher: PAR/NYC
Designer: Noreen M. Lamb
Layout: Louise Lippin
Production Coordinator: Joseph Romano
Cover Illustration: Paul Biniasz
Banner Design: Hrana L. Janto

Creative Director: Harold Steinberg

3 5 7 9 8 6 4 2

Library of Congress Cataloging-in-Publication Data

Lehrer, Brian.
  The Korean Americans.

  (The Peoples of North America)
  Bibliography: p.
  Includes index.
  Summary: Discusses the history, culture, and religion of the Koreans; factors encouraging their emigration, and their acceptance as an ethnic group in North America.
  1. Korean Americans—Juvenile literature.
[1. Korean American] I. Title. II. Series.
E184.K6L45   1988   973'.04957   87-18219
ISBN 0-87754-888-9
     0-7910-0271-3 (pbk.)

Contents

THE PEOPLES OF NORTH AMERICA

CHELSEA HOUSE PUBLISHERS

A
NATION
OF
NATIONS

Daniel Patrick Moynihan

The Constitution of the United States begins: "We the People of the United States . . ." Yet, as we know, the United States is not made up of a single group of people. It is made up of many peoples. Immigrants from Europe, Asia, Africa, and Central and South America settled in North America seeking a new life filled with opportunities unavailable in their homeland. Coming from many nations, they forged one nation and made it their own. More than 100 years ago, Walt Whitman expressed this perception of America as a melting pot: "Here is not merely a nation, but a teeming Nation of nations."

Although the ingenuity and acts of courage of these immigrants, our ancestors, shaped the North American way of life, we sometimes take their contributions for granted. This fine series, *The Peoples of North America,* examines the experiences and contributions of the immigrants and how these contributions determined the future of the United States and Canada.

Immigrants did not abandon their ethnic traditions when they reached the shores of North America. Each ethnic group had its own customs and traditions, and each brought different experiences, accomplishments, skills, values, styles of dress, and tastes in food that lingered long after its arrival. Yet this profusion of differences created a singularity, or bond, among the immigrants.

The United States and Canada are unusual in this respect. Whereas religious and ethnic differences have sparked intolerance throughout the rest of the world—from the 17th-century religious wars to the 19th-century nationalist movements in Europe to the near extermination of the Jewish people under Nazi Germany—North Americans have struggled to learn how to respect each other's differences and live in harmony.

Millions of immigrants from scores of homelands brought diversity to our continent. In a mass migration, some 12 million immigrants passed through the waiting rooms of New York's Ellis Island; thousands more came to the West Coast. At first, these immigrants were welcomed because labor was needed to meet the demands of the Industrial Age. Soon, however, the new immigrants faced the prejudice of earlier immigrants who saw them as a burden on the economy. Legislation was passed to limit immigration. The Chinese Exclusion Act of 1882 was among the first laws closing the doors to the promise of America. The Japanese were also effectively excluded by this law. In 1924, Congress set immigration quotas on a country-by-country basis.

Such prejudices might have triggered war, as they did in Europe, but North Americans chose negotiation and compromise, instead. This determination to resolve differences peacefully has been the hallmark of the peoples of North America.

The remarkable ability of Americans to live together as one people was seriously threatened by the issue of slavery. It was a symptom of growing intolerance in the world. Thousands of settlers from the British Isles had arrived in the colonies as indentured servants, agreeing to work for a specified number of years on farms or as apprentices in return for passage to America and room and board. When the first Africans arrived in the then-British colonies during the 17th century, some colonists thought that they too should be treated as indentured servants. Eventually, the question of whether the Africans should be viewed as indentured, like the English, or as slaves who could be owned for life, was considered in a Maryland court. The court's calamitous decree held that blacks were slaves bound to lifelong servitude, and so were their children.

America went through a time of moral examination and civil war before it finally freed African slaves and their descendants. The principle that all people are created equal had faced its greatest challenge and survived.

Yet the court ruling that set blacks apart from other races fanned flames of discrimination that burned long after slavery was abolished—and that still flicker today. The concept of racism had existed for centuries in countries throughout the world. For instance, when the Manchus conquered China in the 13th century, they decreed that Chinese and Manchus could not intermarry. To impress their superiority on the conquered Chinese, the Manchus ordered all Chinese men to wear their hair in a long braid called a queue.

By the 19th century, some intellectuals took up the banner of racism, citing Charles Darwin. Darwin's scientific studies hypothesized that highly evolved animals were dominant over other animals. Some advocates of this theory applied it to humans, asserting that certain races were more highly evolved than others and thus were superior.

This philosophy served as the basis for a new form of discrimination, not only against nonwhite people but also against various ethnic groups. Asians faced harsh discrimination and were depicted by popular 19th-century newspaper cartoonists as depraved, degenerate, and deficient in intelligence. When the Irish flooded American cities to escape the famine in Ireland, the cartoonists caricatured the typical "Paddy" (a common term for Irish immigrants) as an apelike creature with jutting jaw and sloping forehead.

By the 20th century, racism and ethnic prejudice had given rise to virulent theories of a Northern European master race. When Adolf Hitler came to power in Germany in 1933, he popularized the notion of Aryan supremacy. "Aryan," a term referring to the Indo-European races, was applied to so-called superior physical characteristics such as blond hair, blue eyes, and delicate facial features. Anyone with darker and heavier features was considered inferior. Buttressed by these theories, the German Nazi state from

1933 to 1945 set out to destroy European Jews, along with Poles, Russians, and other groups considered inferior. It nearly succeeded. Millions of these people were exterminated.

The tragedies brought on by ethnic and racial intolerance throughout the world demonstrate the importance of North America's efforts to create a society free of prejudice and inequality.

A relatively recent example of the New World's desire to resolve ethnic friction nonviolently is the solution the Canadians found to a conflict between two ethnic groups. A long-standing dispute as to whether Canadian culture was properly English or French resurfaced in the mid-1960s, dividing the peoples of the French-speaking Quebec Province from those of the English-speaking provinces. Relations grew tense, then bitter, then violent. The Royal Commission on Bilingualism and Biculturalism was established to study the growing crisis and to propose measures to ease the tensions. As a result of the commission's recommendations, all official documents and statements from the national government's capital at Ottawa are now issued in both French and English, and bilingual education is encouraged.

The year 1980 marked a coming of age for the United States's ethnic heritage. For the first time, the U.S. Census asked people about their ethnic background. Americans chose from more than 100 groups, including French Basque, Spanish Basque, French Canadian, Afro-American, Peruvian, Armenian, Chinese, and Japanese. The ethnic group with the largest response was English (49.6 million). More than 100 million Americans claimed ancestors from the British Isles, which includes England, Ireland, Wales, and Scotland. There were almost as many Germans (49.2 million) as English. The Irish-American population (40.2 million) was third, but the next largest ethnic group, the Afro-Americans, was a distant fourth (21 million). There was a sizable group of French ancestry (13 million), as well as of Italian (12 million). Poles, Dutch, Swedes, Norwegians, and Russians followed. These groups, and other smaller ones, represent the wondrous profusion of ethnic influences in North America.

Canada, too, has learned more about the diversity of its population. Studies conducted during the French/English conflict showed that Canadians were descended from Ukrainians, Germans, Italians, Chinese, Japanese, native Indians, and Eskimos, among others. Canada found it had no ethnic majority, although nearly half of its immigrant population had come from the British Isles. Canada, like the United States, is a land of immigrants for whom mutual tolerance is a matter of reason as well as principle.

The people of North America are the descendants of one of the greatest migrations in history. And that migration is not over. Koreans, Vietnamese, Nicaraguans, Cubans, and many others are heading for the shores of North America in large numbers. This mix of cultures shapes every aspect of our lives. To understand ourselves, we must know something about our diverse ethnic ancestry. Nothing so defines the North American nations as the motto on the Great Seal of the United States: *E Pluribus Unum*—Out of Many, One. ∾

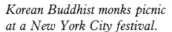
Korean Buddhist monks picnic at a New York City festival.

A PERSEVERING PEOPLE

Korean Americans have been virtually unknown in the United States for most of this century, but in the mid-1960s immigrants from South Korea began settling throughout the country, clustering in and near two major cities on either coast—New York and Los Angeles. Long subjected to anti-Asian immigration legislation, Koreans first were barred from entering the United States and then were allowed in under a strict immigration quota that limited the number of arrivals to 100 per year. This quota system was finally abolished in 1965, and for the first time in nearly four decades, Koreans once again could immigrate freely to U.S. shores. By the late 1960s, a population of several thousand South Koreans suddenly grew to tens, then hundreds of thousands—finally, it seemed that each airliner arriving from Seoul brought another immigrant family to the United States.

South Koreans come to New York and Los Angeles at such a rate that not even the U.S. Census Bureau can keep track of them. In 1980 the official number of Korean Americans was set at 354,000, but some experts, including the Korean Association of New York, argue that the Korean population of Los Angeles alone equals that number and estimate that as many as 1 million people of Korean ancestry now inhabit the country, many of them in cities, including Chicago, El Paso, and Philadelphia.

Today, neighborhoods all over New York and Los Angeles feature Korean produce stores, restaurants, stationery shops, and dry cleaners. Until recently, though, few Korean-owned businesses were visible in bustling downtown neighborhoods; they were confined, instead, to boarded-up and abandoned storefronts. With characteristic determination, Korean Americans went to work, sometimes for 20 hours a day, scrubbing, painting, and stocking their new shops. They refurbished first a single building, then a whole block, and ultimately—in the case of Los Angeles's Koreatown—an entire neighborhood.

In New York City hundreds of moldering "corner stores" were transformed into gleaming greengroceries that often stayed open 24 hours a day and offered produce superior to that available in large supermarkets. Korean Americans rose at dawn and drove their vans to wholesale markets, choosing only the greenest lettuce and crispest apples to resell to customers. Soon they had revolutionized the fruit and vegetable industry in

Korean-American greengrocers are a fixture of New York City streets.

the city and established themselves as major competition for chain stores 10 times their size.

The 600 greengroceries that opened between 1970 and 1980 in the New York metropolitan area filled a growing consumer demand for healthy and natural food. The grocers' uncanny ability to spot commercial opportunities led many to install fresh salad bars in their stores, a convenience for harried New Yorkers who frequently rushed in to grab a quick lunch or dinner.

Not all their fellow Americans, however, greeted Korean immigrants with such enthusiasm. Many watched with bitterness as Korean shopkeepers prospered in the very storefronts where local merchants had gone broke. Korean-American industriousness irked these longtime inhabitants, who perceived the newcomers as parasites who drained poor neighborhoods of cash and returned nothing to the community. This resentment often hardened into racism, and Korean-Americans found themselves victimized by hostile blacks and whites.

Racially motivated hatred was nothing new to Korean Americans. Their earliest days in the United States—at the beginning of this century—had been marred by eruptions of anti-Asian gang violence and by discriminatory legislation approved by state and national governments. In 1906, for instance, Korean-American children suffered with those of Japanese and Chinese heritage when a San Francisco judge ruled that Asian students could not attend public schools in white districts.

Despite these indignities, Korean immigrants remained in the United States. Returning to their old country would have meant even worse hardship. Since the end of the Sino-Japanese War in 1895, troops of Japanese soldiers had dictated the fates of Korean civilians. Their cruelty toward the native population equaled that of any occupying force in history: Japanese stole Korea's vital rice crop, forced its people into heavy labor, and even insisted that they adopt Japanese surnames.

Korea's occupation had resulted from a long-running struggle between major powers for control of the peninsula. In the 16th century, the Japanese vied with the Chinese; in the early 20th century, the Russians entered the fray. All three nations coveted Korea because of its proximity to trade routes and because of its accessible harbors. Years of conflict heightened their perception of the country as a prize whose possession meant supremacy in the Pacific.

By 1905 Japan was the acknowledged victor, though its domination of Korea ended with the close of World War II. The "Land of Morning Calm" (as Korea is called) then became the victim of yet another power struggle between two stronger countries, the United States and the Soviet Union. One consequence of this latest contest is that Korea has been divided into two independent nations: The northern half of the country,

By 1900 Japanese soldiers had become a regular sight in Korea's capital, Seoul, and throughout the country.

controlled by the Soviet Union, is now known as the Democratic People's Republic of Korea, or North Korea. Beneath the 38th parallel, which bisects the peninsula, lies the Republic of Korea, called South Korea—a recently modernized state dependent on U.S. military support.

For South Koreans America seems a land of opportunity, although they sometimes resent the power of the United States to influence their domestic politics. A 1979 poll taken by a leading newspaper in Seoul, the nation's capital, revealed that 50 percent of the population, if given the chance, would consider moving to America. The feelings of South Koreans about the United States are perhaps summed up best by a Korean-American minister in Los Angeles who said, "Jews go to Jerusalem, Koreans go to the United States. America stands for freedom, liberty, and security."

Most of the 20,000–30,000 South Koreans who immigrate annually to this country would probably agree with this remark. In time their offspring—second and third generations born in the United States—will outnumber new arrivals. These Korean Americans will likely embody the New World virtues of independence and informality and also the values of their native land—a unique mix of traditions that gives them a special place amid the many ethnic groups living in North America. ∾

Nearly 20,000 South Korean troops displayed their might in an Armed Forces Day parade in 1963, ten years after the Korean War.

Members of the Korean Embassy to the United States sit for a group photograph near the turn of the century.

A BRIEF HISTORY OF KOREA

Most of Korea is located on a mountainous peninsula about 525 miles long and 125 to 200 miles wide. It juts southeast of Manchuria, the northeastern tip of China, and reaches toward Japan. The proximity of these two powerful neighbors has proved both a blessing and a curse to Koreans. They have benefited from the cultural and scientific advances made by China and Japan but have also suffered repeated military attacks from both.

Korea's documented history begins with a Chinese scholar, Ki-tze, who founded a colony at Pyongyang, in what is now North Korea. But no native Korean state existed until the 1st century A.D., when the kingdom of Koguryo arose near the Yalu River, on the Chinese border. In southern Korea two other kingdoms, Paekche and Silla, subsequently evolved, ushering in the "Three Kingdoms" era. It lasted until 669, when, after a long series of violent struggles, Korea was united for the first time under the flag of Silla, which had been backed by China's T'ang dynasty.

19

During the early years of their unification, Koreans emulated the literature, architecture, costume, and music of the Chinese. They also adopted that country's language in government documents and in the sacred texts of Buddhism, a religion that came from China to Korea in the 6th century.

The period of Silla rule ended in 936 with a bloodless takeover led by a general who established the Koryu dynasty (hence the name Korea). Its monarchs granted land and slaves to local Buddhist monasteries in order to obtain blessings and the promise of eternal happiness. In agrarian Korea, land was a primary source of wealth. As the monasteries expanded their holdings, they gained political influence. Soon the priests' authority rivaled that of the country's aristocracy, and many holy men were seduced by worldly riches and power. Exploiting their privileged status,

Two ancient representations of the Indian prophet Buddha are carved into a stone mountainside.

they shielded themselves from the intervention of Koryu monarchs by citing Buddhist tenets forbidding state intervention in church affairs. The priests' growing corruption went unchecked until 1393, when Korean general Yi Song-gye staged a coup d'état and established a new regime.

Yi's takeover amounted to a war against the priests. He stripped them of authority by seizing their land (as well as the serfs forced to work it) and by changing the state religion from Buddhism to another system, neo-Confucianism. Neo-Confucianism was neither a religion nor a philosophy, but an all-encompassing way of life that emphasized each individual's sense of duty and responsibility to family members and, by extension, to society at large. In contrast to the emphasis on afterlife

Before the Yi takeover in 1388, Buddhist priests lived lavishly, disdaining humble country monasteries such as these.

Nineteenth-century industrial powers eyed Korea's ports as convenient stopovers for their China-bound ships.

and immortality that are found in Buddha's teachings, Confucius's 6th-century B.C. book *High Learning* states, "Give me mortality and nothing else is necessary; without virtue there would be no government, no ruler, and no society." A later Chinese philosopher, Chu Hsi, reinterpreted traditional Confucianism during the late 12th century. His followers viewed personal relationships as belonging to one of five categories: husband and wife; age and youth; friend and friend; father and son; subject and sovereign. These roles were believed to echo an existing natural order. By fulfilling them well, people believed they would bring harmony to human society. Because many Neo-Confucian relationships were hierarchical, the respect shown by subordinates to their superiors took on heightened importance and often led to elaborate, even ritualized, expressions of reverence:

> Though this frame should die and die,
>   though I die a hundred times,
> My bleached bones all turn to dust,
>   my very soul exist or not—
> What can change the undivided heart
>   that glows with faith toward my lord?
>   —Chong Mongju (1337–92),
>   translated by Richard Rutt

The humble adoration individual subjects felt for their sovereign was shared by the nation as a whole. Koreans saw their monarch as a father who, by his virtuous conduct, could guide them toward the fulfillment of their Confucian duties. And on the matter of foreign policy, Koreans regarded themselves as a young nation that could prosper by following the example of China, an older, more experienced country.

During the early years of Yi rule in the 15th century, Koreans emulated China's Ming dynasty much as their Silla ancestors had admired and followed the ways of the T'ang. In principle, Korea ruled its own affairs without Chinese interference, except in cases of national emergency, such as the Japanese invasion of 1592. In practice, the same Ming soldiers who thwarted Japan's 16th-century attack needlessly prolonged their stay on the peninsula and took advantage of their power by appropriating much of the nation's rice crop.

China and Japan

Although China alternated between advising Korea and controlling it, the relationship between the countries did not deteriorate into one of simple exploitation: Chinese monarchs never lost sight of the Confucian principles that guided their dealings with Korea. In contrast, the policy Japan followed was informed purely by colonial ambition—it coveted Korea as a market for its products and as an untapped well of natural resources.

For two centuries China and Japan vied for supremacy in Asia and their struggle sparked a battle for control of the Korean peninsula. The Sino-Japanese War (1894–95) broke China's hardened grip on the area, but Japan still hadn't won the implicit prize, domination of the Pacific. Its new rivals for power in the region—the industrial Western nations of Great Britain, France, and the United States—would prove more formidable than the ailing Chinese empire.

Western Involvement

Long before the Sino-Japanese war, European nations already had begun to parcel bits of China to themselves. They then began to compete for colonies throughout the Pacific region and inevitably took interest in the small peninsula of Korea. But Korea, long isolated from contact with any country but China, shied away from dealing with Westerners—who called it the "Hermit Kingdom"—and officially closed its doors to all non-Chinese foreigners in 1866.

Korea's policy was not unwarranted. It had watched as the United States pressured Japan into a trade agreement in 1854, and as Franco-British forces occupied the ancient Chinese city of Beijing (Peking) in 1860. One by one Asian powers were yielding to industrialized nations and Korea's distaste for the West sharpened into dread.

Not surprisingly, Korea's early encounters with the United States were hostile. In the summer of 1870, an American merchant ship, the USS *General Sherman*, sailed up the Taedong River, in defiance of the Yi government, to force the Koreans into a trade treaty. Alarmed by the sight of a U.S. battleship, a Korean boat fired at the *Sherman* and sank it. This victory for

Korean isolationism did not go unavenged. A year later five U.S. warships anchored near Korea's Kanghwa Island and sent combat troops ashore. But they too were repulsed by native forces.

Korea's independence was short-lived, however. By 1876 colonization was in full swing: the Japanese had pried open the closed doors of the Hermit Kingdom, and, in 1882, just 12 years after the USS *General Sherman* was sunk, Korea reluctantly entered into trade with the United States.

Missionaries

Although Korean rulers disdained foreign influences, their subjects were attracted to some aspects of Western culture, especially its religion. Christianity had been

A U.S. Marine poses with a Korean flag captured during the first "war" between the peninsula and the United States, in 1871.

In 1894 Japanese troops captured Pyongyang, Korea.

known on the peninsula since the 18th century when a Korean, Yi Sung-hun, journeyed to China and, after meeting Catholic missionaries, was converted by them. Upon his return to Korea, he spread the new faith and was soon aided by Catholic priests who joined him in his efforts at wide-scale conversion. By 1865 they had amassed a following of 23,000.

Korea's leader—or Taewon'gun—resented the intrusion of European clerics into his kingdom. In 1866, under royal orders, his troops rounded up and executed a total of 12 priests and 8,000 Korean Catholics. But this slaughter did not deter a second wave of Christians, this time American Protestants, from entering Korea at the end of the 19th century. This new breed of religious workers intended to introduce democracy, as well as Methodism and Presbyterianism, into Korea. They performed their mission through education, establishing schools, including Korea's first medical college, for people of all social classes.

The missionaries' stay in Korea spanned a period of national turmoil when Japanese troops invaded and occupied the peninsula after their 1895 victory in war with China. Students at American-founded schools fumed at foreign domination of their homeland. Suddenly their classroom lectures about democracy acquired a heightened significance as the seeds of national liberation were planted in pupils' minds. In time these schools became a breeding ground for future leaders of the Korean resistance movement against Japanese rule.

The occupying army despised American missionaries but carefully refrained from harassing citizens of the United States. As their strength in the Pacific in-

At the turn of the 20th century, under the direction of the Japanese, Korea built a railway line linking the cities of Seoul and Pusan.

creased, the Japanese grew bolder and, though still unable to oust foreigners, they tyrannized the Korean people, suppressing their religion and outlawing native customs. In 1896 occupying troops enforced the infamous "bobbed hair order" that required Korean men to sever their traditional Confucian topknot. Some committed suicide rather than follow the command.

Annexation

As the Japanese prepared to add Korea to their empire, their control was challenged by another country that had been eyeing Korea's ports, Russia. The Russians' desire to expand Pacific trade routes threatened Japanese domination of the area and provoked the Russo-Japanese War (1904–05). Japan emerged victorious and a world power. The end of the war was mediated by American president Theodore Roosevelt, who in 1906 was awarded the Nobel Peace Prize in recognition of his efforts.

In Sunday schools, American missionaries taught Korean children the tenets of Christianity.

Workers reel raw silk to prepare it for export in 1923.

Unfortunately, both for his countrymen and later for his cousin Franklin Delano Roosevelt, who would lead the United States against Japan during World War II, Theodore Roosevelt did not recognize that he had helped give rise to a new threat. Japan, having gained unforeseen power, began to assemble a war machine—largely at the expense of Korea, which it officially annexed in 1910.

The Japanese now were free to exploit Korea's natural resources and its labor force. They appropriated nearly half the nation's annual rice crop and forced the traditionally agrarian population into factories: between 1911 and 1945 the number of industrial workers in Ko-

In the photograph, text appears on a wall:

WE KOREAN RACE
WELLCOME
THE AMERICAN
RIGHTEOUS
TLOOPS

Many Thanks!
for Your Troubles,
taking for Koreans.

At the close of World War II, Koreans welcomed American soldiers as their saviors from Japanese oppression.

rea rose from 50,000 to 1,500,000. Reduced to virtual slavery, the Koreans dreamed of liberation. Yet only once, on March 1, 1919, did the nation rise en masse to protest its mistreatment. The "March 1st Movement" was quickly suppressed, however, and the Japanese, though they made superficial concessions to resistance leaders, added 10,000 police to their colonial force.

By the 1930s the Japanese occupation of Korea was a cartoon of colonial fascism. Military leaders ordered Koreans to worship only at Japanese Shinto shrines, to use the Japanese language in all schools, and even to adopt Japanese surnames. Korean writer Yalu Li recalls this period in his memoir *The Yalu Flowers:*

Often I pored over my books until past midnight. My studies were more difficult and consumed more time than of old, for we had to learn a great deal of Japanese, and all our textbooks had been replaced by others written in the Japanese language. History was to be re-learnt altogether; all events which had happened in the time of Korean independence were eliminated because the Korean people were no longer looked upon as a nation with its own history, but rather as an outlying community which should always have paid tribute to the Japanese Empire.

When Japan sided with Nazi Germany during World War II, Koreans were ordered to toil at home in munitions plants and airplane factories or were shipped by the hundreds to Japanese coal mines. Their only hope of liberation lay with an Allied victory. In 1943 the Americans, British, and Chinese met in Cairo to discuss strategy and postwar policy and resolved that if Japan

Townspeople in Russian-occupied Pyongyang, Korea, erect a portrait of the Soviet leader Joseph Stalin in 1947.

South Korea's Syngman Rhee thanks U.S. president Harry Truman for speeding American troops to his country after it was invaded by North Korea.

were defeated, it would have to relinquish all the territory it had acquired after 1894.

On August 15, 1945, the Japanese government unconditionally surrendered to the Allied armies and the so-called Cairo Declaration took effect. After 35 years of tyranny, Korea was free. But freedom, again, proved short-lived; only three weeks after its liberation, the country again became embroiled in a struggle between world powers.

The Two Koreas

Despite its defeat in war with Japan earlier in the century, Russia (by this time called the Union of Soviet Socialist Republics, or the Soviet Union), had retained its desire to control Pacific territory, and on August 9, 1945, it invaded Manchuria and northern Korea. By the following autumn, the Soviets had set up a communist government and installed Kim Il-Sung as leader of a new country, North Korea. In response to the Soviet presence, tens of thousands of Koreans fled south across the 38th parallel, the dividing line between Soviet- and American-held land, and settled in the lower part of the peninsula.

Russians and Americans competed for control of a country that had lacked native leadership for so long it could muster no opposition to outside forces. More than 60 political parties worked at cross-purposes in the late 1940s, and only one—the People's Party led by Syngman Rhee—had any significant following. Eventually Rhee gained U.S. support and became the first president of South Korea, but his efforts to form an independent government were initially blocked by the United States.

During this time the United States and the Soviet Union held several conferences to negotiate Korea's future but reached no compromise. In 1947 the frustrated American government brought the problem before the newly formed United Nations. The UN's Committee for the Unification and Rehabilitation of Korea advised that a Korean democracy be established, and that once it was in place, both U.S. and Soviet troops should withdraw from the country.

By January 1948, Koreans south of the 38th parallel found themselves with the trappings of a republican government—a constitution, a president, and elected officials—all under the control of the United States. In defiance of the UN recommendation, the Soviets set up the People's Republic of Korea, a communist counterpart to the Republic of Korea, in September 1948. The two Koreas coexisted warily, at times antagonistically, until the north took advantage of continued unrest in the south, and launched a surprise invasion on June 25, 1950.

An international force organized by the United Nations resisted the takeover and tried to push the Soviet-backed troops out of the peninsula. They very nearly succeeded, but communist China reinforced northern armies with soldiers and supplies, thus making a Western victory impossible. After three years of continuous warfare, the ancient city of Seoul was reduced to rubble, and neither side had triumphed. Western and Eastern forces both lost their taste for combat. On July 27, 1953 they reached an unhappy compromise, creating a demilitarized zone at the 38th parallel with a Soviet-backed government to the north and an American-backed one to the south.

Korea Today

Since the end of that conflict, the people of South Korea have wrested their nation from the ruins of war and brought it into the modern age, succeeding so well that they call their country's current boom a miracle. In a single generation, a nation that could barely feed its own has become a major force in the world's economy, a transformation that has touched the life of almost every South Korean.

Today illiteracy scarcely exists in the country, the average life expectancy at birth has increased by approximately 16 years, and luxuries unheard of 10 years ago—Hyundai cars, GoldStar television sets, and Samsung VCRs, the country's most important products— are commonplace in many households.

Yet, at a time when they could be enjoying their new prosperity, South Koreans are instead rioting amid clouds of tear gas. A recent poll taken for the government by a leading Seoul newspaper disclosed that 65 percent of the respondents were "dissatisfied" or "very

dissatisfied" with their government, particularly with the regime of Chun Doo Hwan. Since 1980 Chun has led the nation and headed its Democratic Justice party, though many South Koreans find his presidency neither democratic nor just.

A military officer by training, Chun seized power in 1980, a year after the assassination of his predecessor

In October 1950, four months after the start of the Korean War, a Seoul woman stands amid the ruins of her home.

The demilitarized zone separating North and South Korea is a crucial buffer between the two hostile countries.

and mentor, Park Chung Hee, set off a national crisis. Because his coup lacked civilian support, Chun staged an election to legitimize his takeover. In doing so, he further convinced South Koreans that they were in the hands of a military dictator. Since he has assumed office, his authoritarian style has alienated nearly all his countrymen, many of whom assert that Chun finds support only among the South Korean military, the secret police force, and the United States government, the secret police, in particular. Without it, Chun probably would never have retained control of the government.

As a South Korean university professor has noted, "Because Chun lacked legitimacy, he had to build power through money and through violence. This has brought on corruption and the use of the police and security forces to secure his position."

During the 1980s, oppression has enveloped South Korea. As Chun has tightened his grip on the country, resentment toward him has grown. In order to stem a ground swell of opposition, he has assured the South Koreans of a free election in 1988 and promised them

On June 10, 1987, Chun Doo Hwan expected a smooth transfer of presidential power to Roh Tae Woo, chairman of the Democratic Justice Party.

constitutional reforms that would enable them to choose presidential candidates directly instead of through a cumbersome legislative process. Reluctantly, the people have tolerated Chun while looking forward to voting him out of office.

In June 1987, though, Chun announced at a Democratic Justice party convention that he would forestall free elections and instead decide himself who South Korea's next leader would be. Acting as a monarch rather than a president, Chun essentially named Democratic Justice party chairman Roh Tae Woo as his successor, thereby crushing the country's hope of holding free

In 1953 a majority of Koreans still lived in rural poverty.

elections before 1990. After Chun's speech, he and Roh stood before 7,000 of their party's delegates, hands joined and upraised in victory. The next day, South Korea erupted into violence.

The Hyundai Motor Company's "Excel," first introduced in the United States in 1986, was an immediate success.

The Student Movement

The largest furor was created by South Korea's college students. On campuses throughout the nation more than 60,000 students, committed to toppling Chun's regime, confronted military police in the streets, hurling "Molotov cocktails"—gasoline bombs—and rocks. In return, the police fired volleys of acrid tear gas at the crowds.

In June 1987 a dissident in Seoul throws a lit Molotov cocktail during a clash between about 1,000 demonstrators and 2,000 riot police.

Korea's history of student antigovernment violence actually began before World War II, when an opposition movement formed against the Japanese. One of the most famous young patriots of that era, Syngman Rhee, sought exile in the United States and, through his work in Korean-American churches, organized fellow Koreans to fight for national independence. In 1948 he returned home and rode to the presidency in the wake of Japan's defeat by the Americans, only to have his own corrupt regime overthrown by student protesters in 1960.

A New Alliance

Korean students have acted as a national conscience since the days of Japanese occupation. They have not only fought injustice but have also kept alive the promise of independence and democracy during some of the country's darkest hours, including the crises of the 1980s. Chun has tried to discredit student protesters by linking them with the North Korean government, but by 1987 his accusations had fallen on deaf ears. The majority of South Koreans realized that students were less likely to spout communist ideology than to make remarks such as "The Korean people want a president who is elected by the Korean people." Indeed, most of the country's usually apolitical middle class publicly supported the student-led opposition movement, and many political analysts said that Chun had lost his credibility even with this traditional stronghold. According to a 1987 article in the *New York Times*:

> The authoritarian Government here has long accepted on faith that as long as the economy keeps growing and as long as more people define themselves as middle class—acquiring Samsung television sets, Hyundai cars, and GoldStar computers—South Koreans would not risk their gains by taking to the streets in the name of democracy. . . . As affluence has spread, so has a yearning for the rights that often go with it—freedom of assembly, speech, and press, and a desire for a truly civilian Government—something last experienced 27 years ago.

The clouds of tear gas that fouled the air of Korean cities benefited the burgeoning protest movement of mid-1987. Front-page stories filed by journalists from around the world raised sympathy for South Koreans of all classes, who were united in suffering with irritated eyes and lungs. Korean housewives and businessmen put on surgical masks and goggles, marched into the streets of Seoul and Pusan—traditionally the domain of young radicals—and quickly learned the art of dodging tear gas canisters.

By June 1987, demonstrations included as many as 50,000 protesters. The presence of middle-class businessmen in the chanting crowds signaled a dramatic shift in the social makeup of dissidents and drew immediate comment from foreign reporters:

Men, women and children filled the Myongdong Cathedral and spilled over onto a flagstone plaza where they stood in prayer or sat on the ground despite a drenching rainstorm. When the rain stopped, the crowd surged into the street outside, holding candles aloft and singing hymnlike songs of protest. They were held back by thousands of police officers with riot shields stretched before them. . . . For the most part the rally was peaceful, reflecting a growing middle-class component in protests that the Government has characterized as an attempt at "violent revolution."

The Church in South Korea

During this time Seoul's Myongdong Cathedral became a center of antigovernment activity. Candlelight vigils and rallies held there attested to the political concern of yet another segment of South Korean society, the clergy. When 500 protesters locked themselves inside the cathedral to take refuge from riot police, they were protected both by the building's imposing structure and by priests and nuns. As rumors spread that the police might force their way in to arrest protesters, dozens of clerics stepped in their way and formed a protective human chain on the cathedral's main path. They knew that the government, no matter how enraged, would not allow the world press to photograph South Korean riot police pushing nuns to the ground and dragging them into waiting vans. Yet even the clergy was not completely exempt from physical assault. After a special candlelight service to pray for peace, Catholic, Protestant, and Buddhist clergy found themselves confronted by military police on the steps of Myongdong Cathedral and needed to force their way past rows of officers in riot gear.

Christian opposition to the Korean government dates back to American missionaries who introduced Korea's population not only to the spiritual teachings of Jesus Christ but also to advocates of political freedom such as Thomas Paine. The influence of these mission-

Roman Catholic nuns keep a vigil to prevent riot police from attacking students barricaded inside the Myongdong Cathedral in Seoul.

aries has remained in the country since the early 20th century and was clearly in evidence in the June 1987 demonstrations. One young patriot echoed the sentiments of many when he said, "It's not important who becomes president. What's important is the extent to which we can achieve democracy." ∾

In 1919 Korean-American Boy Scouts carry the flags of both their ancestral land and their adopted country.

EARLY KOREAN IMMIGRATION

At the end of the 19th century, during an era of economic, political, and religious upheaval in Korea, the United States received its first refugees from the peninsula, three pro-Japanese activists seeking exile after an unsuccessful attempt to overthrow the government. Like other radical Koreans, the trio who came to America probably learned about the United States through exposure to Christian missionaries. But their flight from home was an isolated incident that bore little relation to the first true wave of immigrants—Koreans who traveled west not to seek political sanctuary but to find work in the fields of Hawaii.

Plantation Life

In the early 1900s, the sugar industry in Hawaii, a U.S. territory that had not yet achieved statehood, was booming, and plantations needed more workers than the native population could supply. The planters had previously recruited thousands of Chinese and Japanese laborers who, like all immigrants, initially accepted low wages. Later, however, plagued by exploitation and discrimination, they abandoned agrarian work in search of better opportunities.

Korean peasants flailing barley face the entrance of Pusan's harbor (circa 1919).

At about the same time, rumor spread among the plantation owners that Koreans were more industrious than either the Chinese or the Japanese, and after consultation with the U.S. ambassador to Korea, recruiters began journeying to the peninsula. The Hawaiian Sugar Planters Association struck a deal with David Deshler, an American businessman living in Korea, who was paid five dollars for every laborer he lured to the Hawaiian islands. Deshler even offered unsuspecting Koreans loans of $100 so they could travel to Hawaii and get settled.

Despite their distrust of Western ways and people, Koreans of the early 1900s found the terms of migration attractive: a monthly wage of $15, free housing, health care, English lessons, and the perennially warm Hawaiian climate. Recruiters in Korea used the upbeat slogan "The country is open—go forward" to portray Hawaii as a land of opportunity. Some churchgoing Koreans learned about the islands through missionaries who argued that life in the West would make them better Christians.

Most recruits intended not to settle permanently in Hawaii but to save their wages and return home as soon as possible. This plan often failed because the cost of living on the islands far exceeded that in Korea, and even with free housing it was very difficult for workers to save their wages.

The first shipload of Koreans, numbering about 100, arrived in Honolulu on January 13, 1903. Most were illiterate farmers eager to escape a lifetime of back-breaking labor in rural villages. Immediately after disembarking they were herded onto sugar plantations and soon resumed the life of daily toil they had known at home. During the next two years, more than 7,000 Koreans followed their countrymen halfway across the Pacific, hoping their fortunes would grow as quickly as the Hawaiian sugar cane.

Like the Chinese and Japanese before them, Koreans in Hawaii found plantation life hard and unreward-

Workers harvest cane on a Hawaiian sugar plantation in the early 1900s.

ing. The sunny weather, described by recruiters as paradisal, proved oppressive. The immigrants were drained by 10-hour workdays and 6-day workweeks. Their exhaustion was not relieved by conditions on the plantation, which invariably included squalid housing, isolation, and poor food. Few had the time or energy to attend the promised English lessons.

In his book *Koreans in America* Bong-youn Choy quotes an immigrant's account of his plantation days in Hawaii:

> I got up at four-thirty in the morning and made my breakfast. I had to be out to the field at five o'clock. I worked 10 hours a day with a 67 cents a day wage. My supervisor . . . was very strict with us. He . . . did not allow us to stand up straight once we started to work. He treated us like cows and horses. We carried our number all the time as an identification card and were never called by name, but by number.

(continued on page 57)

After it was gathered from the fields, sugar was first milled in Hawaii and then transported to refineries in California.

AN ART GALLERY

Classical Korean art often depicted animals such as the dog portrayed in this c. 17th-century painting and this 12th-century ceramic duck. The animal motif recurs in contemporary works: winged pieces sculpted by Korean American Kang Ja Lee and the bird-shaped canvas created by Soonja O. Kim.

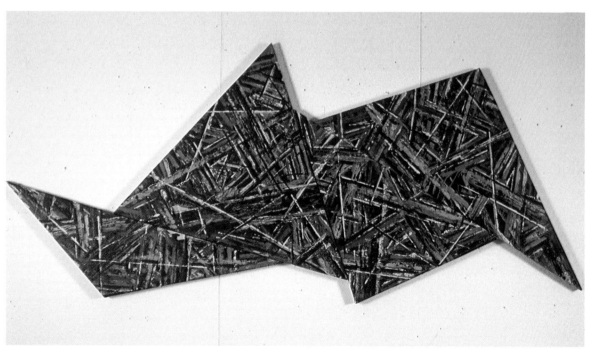

51

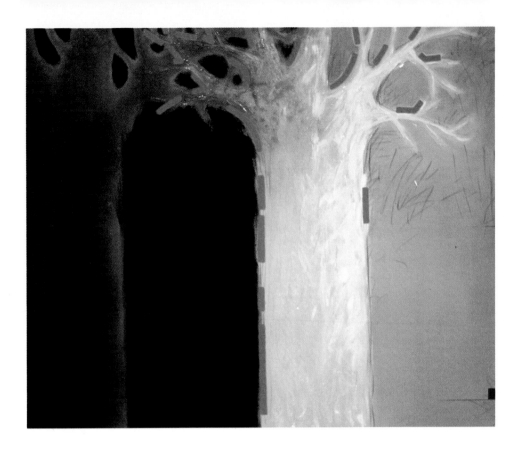

Modern American painting inspires many younger artists to work in the expressionist style, with its bold coloring and abstract images. Some examine Western themes such as the biblical story of Salome, interpreted by Younghee Choi (bottom right). Also shown here (clockwise from left): Jung Hyong Kim's Scattered Plan; an untitled painting by Ku Lim Kim, and Sonia Hahn's Self-Portrait—Confidence.

Today Korean Americans freely air their views at public rallies and in works of art with political or social implications, such as Yong Soon Min's ironic American Friend *and Ik-Joong Kang's conceptual* Time and Toilet Paper.

The creativity of Korean Americans links fine art with high fashion. Here designer Soo Young Lee outfits a model in material that mimics the work of the Dutch painter Piet Mondrian.

(continued from page 48)

Disappointed with their new lives, many immigrants felt deceived by the false promises of their recruiters and refused to repay the $100 loaned them by David Deshler. Because they could not count on Hawaiian officials for leadership or protection, Koreans on the plantations improvised a form of self-government called a *dong-hoe*. Made up of democratically elected councils, dong-hoes helped settle disputes and maintain order among Koreans. Eventually, representatives of all the plantations formed one large representative body, known as the United Korean Society. In addition to creating an independent system of government, Korean immigrants—about a third of whom were Christian—founded churches. Before long, these evolved into community centers that provided companionship and sympathy.

The Mainland

For all their efforts at bettering their lives, Korean plantation hands couldn't change the exploitative nature of work in the sugar fields. Between 1905 and 1910 those who could afford to usually left for Hawaiian cities, finding jobs in seaports or in the Dole Pineapple cannery. Some set up small businesses such as grocery stores, laundries, and tailor shops.

About 2,000 of the original 7,000 immigrants returned to Korea, where conditions were even worse. By 1905 the Japanese had established control of the peninsula and mistreated the civilian population so badly that they were compelled to stop Koreans from fleeing their own country in droves. As the threat of a mass exodus loomed, occupying powers forced the native government to ban emigration. Word of Japanese oppression spread to Hawaii, where immigrants resolved to bear a double burden: improving their lot in the West while fighting for Korea's liberation from Japan. With these new goals in mind, many left the islands for the U.S. mainland.

Koreans settled all across America. Many joined Chinese in railroad jobs, laying tracks throughout the West. Others farmed rice, a crop they had been familiar with in Korea and which flourished in the cooler climate of northern California. Some took up vegetable growing and established their own small farms. Released from the grueling work of the plantations, the immigrants began to look past mere survival and instead dreamed of establishing families. Another obstacle stood in their way, however. Almost no Korean women had come with the first arrivals, and, because the Japanese had outlawed emigration, none were expected.

Picture Brides

Immigrant men wanted to marry women from their homeland, so they followed the lead of Chinese and Japanese in America and mailed pictures of themselves home to matchmakers. If a Korean woman liked a particular man's photograph, she sent him one of herself; if both liked what they saw, the "picture bride" came to the United States. The Japanese government loosened its emigration restriction enough to let 1,000 of these women set off for Western shores.

Many women who had never even traveled outside their villages now set out alone to journey halfway across the Pacific. Upon docking in San Francisco or Honolulu they were met on board by husbands whom they were seeing for the first time in person. The couple would be married before the woman officially entered Hawaii or the United States; the marriage afforded her official status as the wife of a U.S. resident, so she could freely enter the United States or Hawaii and remain indefinitely.

As risky as these marriages were, picture brides preferred wedding a stranger in a new land to continuing a life of unrelieved poverty in Korea. Sometimes, though, they were shocked to find themselves saddled with husbands old enough to be the fathers of the men

they had seen in matchmakers' photographs. In such cases the marriage might end in divorce. More frequently, picture brides soon became picture widows—often with small children. Luckily, all the brides were U.S. residents and therefore could stay in the country no matter how the marriage turned out.

Demoralized by plantation life, many Korean immigrants moved to Honolulu to work in Dole's pineapple canneries.

The First Generation

Picture brides, practically the only Koreans permitted to emigrate from their occupied homeland, saved the Korean population in America. And bleak as their fate might seem today, these women fared reasonably well. Many persuaded their husbands to move from farms to cities where there was higher-paying work and also better education available to their children.

The Confucian belief in scholarship had filtered down through Korean society and affected even those with no access to formal schooling. Although the majority of the immigrants were illiterate, they urged their children to excel in their studies. As a result, many first-generation Korean Americans became doctors, lawyers, and teachers. Korean parents expected their children to master not only the American curriculum but to attend special schools that taught Korea's language and customs.

Young Korean Americans worked hard to succeed in U.S. society while still maintaining their Asian identity, and they felt loyal both to the new land of their birth and to their traditional homeland. Many bristled at their ancestral lands occupation by Japan and vowed to fight for the independence of Korea, a country they had never seen.

The Korean Independence Movement

In the early 1900s, Korean Americans continued the fight for national liberation begun by their parents. Immigrants had formed the *Tae-Han Kungminhoe* (The Korean National Association, or THK) with the aim of

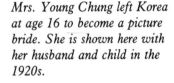

Mrs. Young Chung left Korea at age 16 to become a picture bride. She is shown here with her husband and child in the 1920s.

A Korean-American family poses for a group photograph in Hawaii.

soliciting the help of the U.S. government in freeing Korea, but the United States was more interested in maintaining good relations with the powerful Japanese than in helping the Korean independence movement. The THK dissolved.

In reaction, Koreans adopted a more militant strategy and began training an amateur army on U.S. soil for a planned invasion of Korea. Between 1910 and 1916, they established military academies in California, Nebraska, Missouri, and Wyoming. In the end, though, their great determination could not compensate for the small number of available men. Koreans acknowledged the impossibility of defeating the Japanese occupiers, and, once again, they resorted to diplomatic channels to advance their cause.

Throughout the years of annexation, immigrants and their children donated hard-earned money to groups fighting for Korean liberation. They anxiously followed news of the homeland and vainly urged the indifferent U.S. government to intervene.

Discrimination

Soon after their appearance in the West, Korean immigrants faced a second obstacle to freedom—anti-Asian prejudice, a practice tracing back to the mid-19th century, when Chinese first migrated to the United States. To some Americans the newly arrived Chinese presented such a threat that the term "yellow peril" became widely used. Aversion to Orientals intensified steadily, and in 1882 Congress passed the Chinese Ex-

A 19th-century political cartoon portrays the animosity many second- and third-generation Americans felt toward Asian immigrants.

clusion Act, the only law in U.S. history that prohibited immigration from a specific nation.

Anti-Asian sentiment was most vehement in California, especially in San Francisco, where many immigrants from the Far East settled. The city's white population feared it would lose its political clout and its jobs to Asians willing to toil for slave wages. This prejudice pervaded California's state institutions, and was reinforced first by a 1906 ruling that barred Oriental students from public schools in white districts, and later by the 1913 Webb-Heney Land Law, forbidding Asians to own property. In 1924 racist legislation culminated in the national Oriental Exclusion Act, which banned all Asian immigration to the United States, and remained in effect for nearly 40 years.

Like all Asians, Korean Americans suffered not only institutionalized discrimination but also the hatred of whites whom they met face to face. One immigrant recalled his experience in Los Angeles in 1918:

> I entered a restaurant and sat down in order to have lunch. Although there were not many customers, the waitress did not come to my table. After a while, a young receptionist came to me and said with a low voice, "We can't serve you lunch because if we start serving lunch to Orientals, white Americans will not come here."

Some immigrants were menaced by violent white gangs, yet they rarely fought back or complained to the police, who would label them as "troublemakers." Because their population was much smaller than that of the Chinese and Japanese, Koreans were especially vulnerable to mistreatment. Until midcentury, Korean Americans lived as a minority within a minority, without neighborhoods of their own, lumped together with other Asians by most Americans who knew or cared little about a remote peninsula lying between Japan and China.

Some immigrants, such as Oregon restaurateur H. D. Lee, prospered on the West Coast despite the daily presence of racism.

A New Migration

During the Korean War (1950–1953), American soldiers fought side by side with South Korean troops and also came to know the country's civilian population. Some soldiers fell in love with Korean women, married them, and returned to the United States with their "war brides," the first Korean immigrants legally allowed into the United States since 1924. Before their arrival the entire Korean community consisted of the original 7,000 Hawaiian plantation workers, the picture brides, their descendants, and a few hundred political refugees who had managed to slip out of Korea by posing as students.

The arrival of the war brides began a new era of Korean immigration. The notorious Oriental Exclusion Act ended and was replaced in 1952 by the McCarran-Walter Act, which reopened America's door to Asians. But even this Congressional law, though it acknowledged that it was discriminatory to exclude immigrants solely on the basis of national origin, established a quota system that let into the country only a small fraction of those hoping to immigrate.

The quota of Koreans was set at 100 per year, evidence that the U.S. government still bridled at the idea of a mass migration from the East. Many Koreans despaired of ever reaching America. At last, Congress passed the 1965 Immigration and Nationality Act. This legislation replaced the quotas with a "preference system" that gave precedence to immigration applications from the relatives of U.S. citizens and from professionals with skills needed in the United States. Thousands of South Korean doctors and nurses rushed to take advantage of the new law, were quickly admitted to the United States, and found work in understaffed inner-city hospitals. They were soon joined by others with backgrounds in science or technology.

Unlike the Korean laborers who had toiled under the Hawaiian sun, these newcomers (and others like them from India and the Philippines) came from upper-class families with an open invitation to the United States. Their higher status seemed to differentiate them from earlier immigrants who could find only the most menial work on farms or in factories, jobs that most Americans disdained. In reality, both groups filled a demand for labor: The wave that arrived at the beginning of the century supported a revolution in industry; those who came later aided one in technology.

Relatives

By passing the 1965 Immigration and Nationality Act, American lawmakers intended to filter out all but a foreign elite. But when Korean professionals arrived in America, they spotted provisions of the new law that allowed U.S. citizens to bring their relatives to the United States. Lawmakers watched in dismay as hus-

Volunteers from the Korean Women's Relief Society wrap surgical instruments for shipment to South Korea in 1951.

bands, wives, parents, siblings, and cousins of the newly naturalized immigrants poured in. Soon, the majority of Koreans in the country were no longer the desired professionals, but their family members—some of whom were unskilled.

Today, relatives of U.S. citizens compose the largest group of immigrants coming from South Korea to the United States. Most leave their land after being squeezed out of jobs and housing in Seoul, a city with 9.5 million inhabitants. Alarmed by overcrowding, the South Korean government encourages emigration and works closely with U.S. officials in Seoul to arrange for immigrant visas, which can take as long as five years to obtain.

Overpopulation, however, is not the only reason for South Korean immigration to America. The chance to earn a better living, and, at the same time, to flee the regimes of U.S.-backed military dictators, is what attracts most of those who depart for the West. Political repression is endemic to Korean politics. Any opponents of the current president, Chun Doo Hwan, find themselves under the surveillance of the notorious Korean Central Intelligence Agency (KCIA). One dissenter from the current regime, a Korean-American lawyer, told of an incident that frightened him into leaving his native country:

> I had a friend working on government statistics for a
> major bank in Seoul. Once, he went to a holiday party
> and discussed how the statistics are gathered. He
> disappeared that night. Six months later he was found
> in the custody of the KCIA. He was badly beaten
> and psychologically damaged.

Even though South Koreans resent the presence of the U.S. government, they are drawn to America because of its luxuries. Portable cassette recorders and stylish clothing are frequently smuggled out of American military bases and sold on the black market. And television

shows like "Dallas" and "Dynasty" reinforce a mythical image of the United States as a land of riches.

Upon arriving on U.S. soil, Koreans realize that not all Americans lead opulent lives, but many newcomers remain determined to succeed in this country. Almost all Korean Americans distinguish themselves through their tireless work and devotion to their families—traits that their new compatriots view with admiration. ✎

In 1951 Korean war bride Yong Soon Morgan is greeted by her new in-laws upon arriving in the United States with her husband, a U.S. Army sergeant.

Michael Yu owns a kosher deli in Jamaica, New York.

THE NEW WORLD

Like their predecessors in the Hawaiian sugarcane fields, Korean immigrants of the mid-1960s left their homeland for the chance to earn a good living. But unlike the first wave (who had planned to make their bundle and return home), the later arrivals—a privileged group of professionals—wanted to blend fully into American society. They avoided the urban experience of earlier generations by bypassing the small ethnic enclaves that were the traditional home of immigrants in favor of comfortable suburbs that represented the good life in America.

A majority of the newcomers were doctors who helped ease the national shortage of physicians. They settled near Los Angeles and New York City, urban areas with large populations of poor people and an enormous demand for medical workers. By the early 1970s, Koreans and other Asians often staffed inner-city hospitals avoided by American doctors. This influx of Korean, Indian, and Filipino doctors rescued hundreds of overcrowded facilities.

Many native-born physicians, however, objected to the idea of Asians treating hospital patients, especially those with mental rather than physical illnesses. Their concern was not unfounded. For example, during the 1970s, foreign doctors who found jobs spurned by their non-Asian colleagues in New York's state psychiatric hospitals frequently proved unable to diagnose their pa-

69

tients accurately. In her investigative study of the Creedmore State Hospital, *Is There No Place on Earth for Me,* author Susan Sheehan writes:

> In 1978, two psychiatrists alternated admission screenings in the Clearview unit—Dr. Shamaldaree Batra and Dr. Sun Ming Wong, the psychiatrist who had discharged Miss Frumkin [the patient] on May 31 as a "he." It was Dr. Sun's turn to do an admission screening. . . . Dr. Sun was a 35-year-old native of Taiwan who had received his medical degree in Taipei, and had come to the United States in 1973. . . . More than one person . . . who later happened to read Dr. Sun's mental status report was surprised that he . . . had failed to elicit any delusions or auditory hallucinations from Miss Frumkin, but, as Dr. Sun later acknowledged, he didn't recognize the names Mary Poppins, Don Knotts, Peter Lawford, and Lou Costello, and he hadn't understood that Miss Frumkin had said anything about making movies with these people, whoever they were.

Defenders of Asian doctors argued that the medical licensing examinations for physicians trained abroad were at least as rigorous as those given to American medical students. In addition, they pointed out that without Asian physicians many hospitals would have closed.

Relative Newcomers

In time Korean professionals gained acceptance both in the medical community and in the middle-class neighborhoods where they had settled. Their rapid assimilation made their lot easier, but often it left them lonely for the companionship of fellow Koreans.

Once they earned American citizenship, many Korean immigrants sponsored the immigration of family members who wanted to join them in the United States. Soon their relatives were pouring in at such a rate that the 1965 Immigration and Nationality Act was infor-

mally dubbed the "Brothers and Sisters Act." Although the U.S. government looked askance at these newcomers—many of whom were poor and intentionally excluded by the rigid 1965 guidelines—no legal means existed for keeping them out. As relatives of U.S. citizens, they were entitled to settle here and even to become naturalized Americans themselves. The criterion for gaining entry into the United States had been subtly reversed—immigrants were allowed in on the basis of their own needs, not those dictated by the shifting U.S. economy.

Since 1972 a majority of the approximately 20,000 Koreans arriving annually in the United States have been brought over by their relatives. Nearly half of

President Lyndon Johnson chose the historic site of Liberty Island for the signing of the liberalized U.S. Immigration Act on October 4, 1965.

The second wave of Korean immigration actually began at the close of the Korean War when the wives and children of American servicemen entered the United States.

these have made their home in Los Angeles's "Korea-town," an area just west of the city's downtown. Once a deteriorating neighborhood, Koreatown has been re-vitalized by immigrants who have renovated its resi-dential and commercial districts, and it is now home to at least 150,000 Korean Americans. New York City has equivalent areas in Flushing, Woodside, and Jackson Heights, all in the borough of Queens, which contains a majority of the city's estimated 200,000 Korean Amer-icans and immigrants.

Although far from destitute (one-way plane fare from Seoul cost about $1,000 in 1987), many newcom-ers do not belong to a social elite as did the first wave of post-1965 professionals. Korean Americans them-selves rigorously categorize one another by their posi-tion on the different rungs of their social ladder: on top are descendants of the first wave of immigrants (most of whom reside in Hawaii); second come the post-1965 wave of doctors and technicians; last are the relatives who followed the professionals. This final group is often snubbed by more assimilated and affluent countrymen. The son of a research physicist told an interviewer:

> Most Koreans I know and keep friendly with are professionals, scattered around the city. They avoid the Korean neighborhoods. The people living together in the neighborhoods are from lower-class backgrounds. Back home my family would not mix with such people. Even if they do get lucky and make money, they are still essentially lower class. No education, no sophistica-tion. There are no facets in their personality. They can't carry on a conversation. Some people can only make money. I have much more in common with a native New Yorker than with a Korean greengrocer.

Snobbery within the Korean-American community saddens many of its members. Wistfully comparing themselves with the Chinese, who seem united by a national identity, they try to uncover the source of this elitism. One Korean American remarked, "If I were in a room full of people and there were one or two Koreans I would not feel closer to the Koreans. That is what the Japanese did to us. They made us strangers to each other." Sociologists have pinpointed this discord among Koreans as one of several causes of the distress that haunts the immigrant community in the form of high divorce rates, suicide, and mental illness. Unhappiness, it seems, often accompanies Korean Americans' heroic efforts to succeed.

Many immigrants feel pressured to demonstrate their upward mobility and their reputation as "super immigrants." Magazine and newspaper articles often sentimentalize "Korean industriousness" as a throwback to the golden days of the American melting pot. Even though non-Asian Americans admire Korean newcomers, their esteem is sometimes tinged with suspicion, as though they cannot figure out what the Koreans are "really" doing here. The name of Sun Myung Moon, leader of the controversial Unification Church, sometimes surfaces in conversations about Koreans in America. Aware of this undesirable association, many Korean Americans fight being labeled "Moonies" and

Unlike their predecessors at the turn of the century, later immigrants from Korea were anxious to be assimilated into American culture.

Those with enough capital to begin dry-cleaning shops are considered fortunate in the Korean-American community.

take pains to distance themselves from his cult. One greengrocer in New York City hangs a "Moonies not Welcome" sign in his store window.

Although current anti-Asian sentiment does not approach the "yellow peril" hysteria of the 19th century, it still hinders the progress of some immigrants. Congressional legislation now prohibits discrimination based on national origin or race, but bias against Asians is often subtle, and therefore difficult to contest in court. Korean Americans frequently say that employers praise their hard work but pass them over for management positions in professional and technical jobs—assertions confirmed by U.S. government statistics. Even Korean students feel themselves straining against an invisible quota when they apply to colleges. They assert that the flood of excellent applicants has made prestigious universities like Stanford and Massachusetts Institute of Technology wary of becoming "too Asian."

The Greengrocers

Unlike other first-generation Americans, Koreans struggling to enter the country's top schools often are the offspring of highly educated parents. Even those recent immigrants scorned for being provincial and mercantile by more assimilated Koreans frequently hold graduate degrees in engineering, education, architecture, and other professions.

After entering the United States, they suddenly find themselves washing vegetables, arranging candy bar displays, and counting change for a living because they lack fluency in English and have no network of professional contacts. Small retail shops that require little capital to open enable them to support themselves and their families.

In Chicago, an estimated 95 percent of all dry-cleaning stores have Korean owners, whereas immigrants in New York, Los Angeles, and El Paso prefer import-export businesses when they can afford to operate them. Korean-run groceries have become a fixture in New York City. Most neighborhoods can claim at least one. Business districts often have several on each block. Many of these enterprises began like Ki Kang's.

Hochan Kim's clothing store was one of the first Korean-owned businesses in downtown El Paso, Texas.

One hundred twenty-five Korean-Americans, including this girl, participated in a group naturalization ceremony in Collegeville, Pennsylvania.

After immigrating to the United States in 1969, Mr. Kang soon found a job in his own profession (engineering) but realized that his poor English would keep him from winning a promotion. During this time his wife opened a small produce store, and Mr. Kang discovered that the family fortune lay in grocery selling, not engineering. He traded his three-piece suit for a white apron and joined Mrs. Kang behind the cash register. The couple expanded their store, bought a second

one, and eventually owned the building that housed it, thus establishing themselves as landlords as well as greengrocers. The Kangs' skill at parlaying a small investment into a profitable business exemplifies the industriousness of Korean Americans and their ability to see opportunity where others can't.

Entrepreneurs

Intent on starting their own businesses, Korean immigrants of the 1970s tolerated extraordinarily difficult, even dangerous, working conditions. Many took over shops in high-crime neighborhoods that had been deserted by other merchants. New Yorker Jong Chul Lee remembers his first store:

> I found a space next to a fish market on Belmont Avenue in Brooklyn. It used to be a butcher shop and no one wanted it because it still smelled so badly of meat. So I got it cheap and two other guys and I fixed up just the front, where we sold general merchandise. Gradually we fixed up the rest of it and opened the store little by little. Some days we worked all day long and made only $20. And guys used to hang around waiting to steal things. But luckily we had good protection from the police. Finally, we moved the store to a better location.

Today, Jong Chul Lee owns a firm that imports handbags from Korea, and he is president of New York City's Korean Businessmen's Association. Though he credits his current success to his ability to work hard and save money, Mr. Lee probably would admit that his greatest resource was not financial, but cultural. As a people, Koreans are both adapters and survivors. Centuries of political and economic hardship have taught them that change comes only through struggle and patience. Without the traits of tolerance and practicality, learned early in life, Korean immigrants might never have endured their pilgrimage to the cities of America.

As they cope with their sometimes difficult lives there, they gain support from traditional Korean values and customs.

Many recent immigrants, for example, employ an ancient Korean loan system involving a *kye*, a sum of money shared among a group of business owners. Typically, a new greengrocer will be allowed to use the kye for a year and keep whatever profits he has made. He must then pass the kye to the next person. This system is used not only to finance new businesses but also to boost the owner of a greengrocery, a store requiring 16-hour workdays without a weekend break, into a more pleasant and profitable type of store, such as a dry-cleaning shop.

Many Korean Americans measure their success by the type of business they own. Most grocery and general merchandise stores yield the smallest profits; dry cleaning is easier and usually more lucrative; and stationery shops, beauty salons, and furniture stores—the cleanest and easiest to run—are widely viewed as the most desirable of all. Most Korean merchants view each business as a stepping stone to the next and prefer not to operate their original store for long.

Education: Key to the Future

Korean-American ambition extends to the youngest generation, whose scholastic excellence has been well documented in school systems across the United States. Education has been crucial to Korean families for centuries. In the past, a career in the civil service—the route to success in traditional society—customarily began with notoriously difficult qualifying examinations, each requiring several months of study. Today, Korean-American parents monitor their children's academic performance and often demand a discipline and dedication unknown in most American households. One Korean-American parent noted the difference in expectations:

Markets such as this one line Olympic Boulevard, the main thoroughfare of Los Angeles's Koreatown.

My wife and I check our daughter's assignments every day to make sure everything is done and done well. We review her tests, too. I think Korean parents place a lot more pressure on their kids.

Like other Asians, Koreans seem especially talented in math and science, and many families encourage the study of these fields, which they regard as a sure path to upward mobility. Recently, young Korean Americans have joined Chinese-American teenagers in sweep-

ing the prizes awarded annually in the Westinghouse Electric Corporation science scholarship competition, a nationwide talent search for high school students.

In 1986 high school senior Carl Hyun-suk Park was nominated as a finalist for the Westinghouse competition. His project in biology included research conducted at New York University and the New York Aquarium, where he studied the physiology of animal cells. A year later another Korean American, Hyong Yoon Park, also was named a finalist for creating a new series of complex organic chemical compounds in his own laboratory at the City College of New York.

Despite their reputation for excellence in math and science, not all Korean Americans enter technical fields.

The Reverend Sun Myung Moon married 2,200 couples in a mass wedding at New York's Madison Square Garden in 1982.

One notable exception is Korean-born Nam June Paik, a world-famous video artist who was one of 86 immigrants presented with a Liberty Award as part of the 1986 Statue of Liberty Centennial. Paik fled war-torn Seoul with his family in 1950, when he was 18 years old. His parents made their way first to Hong Kong, and later to Tokyo, where they settled. As a college student at the university there, Paik earned a degree in philosophy and, through his study of aesthetics, came under the influence of avant-garde Western culture.

Paik decided to emigrate but didn't join the population of professional Koreans flooding into the United States. "Many middle-class Koreans went to live in America in the 1950s," he later told an interviewer.

Hyong Yoon Park, a winner of the 1987 Westinghouse Science Talent Search competition, demonstrates the structure of the new organic chemical compounds he synthesized.

"But I think there is not much culture in America." Instead, he traveled to West Germany to study music. There he met the American composer John Cage and soon realized that America was not the artistic wasteland he had once imagined. "I hear about Robert Rauschenberg [a contemporary artist], and about other artists doing new things in New York. I think, 'Slowly, slowly, America is coming up.' " When Paik finally arrived in 1964 to see New York for himself, he found it "as dirty as Paris and as ugly as Düsseldorf." Nevertheless, he stayed and in 1976 became a U.S. citizen.

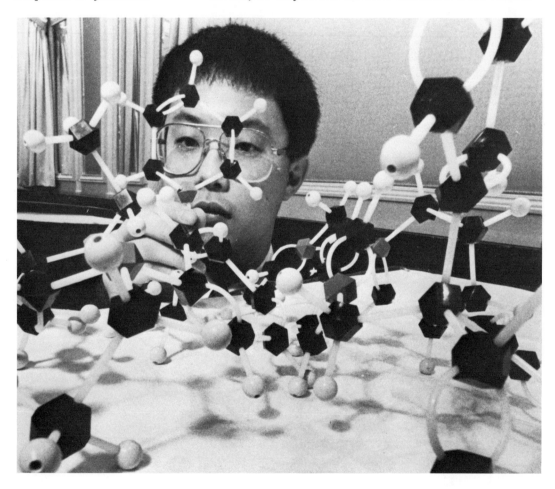

Now Paik lives in a converted warehouse in the New York City neighborhood of SoHo, long an artists' community. According to *Time* magazine:

> Paik's cavernous loft resembles a Sony factory that was
> in the process of being ransacked by terrorists when
> an earthquake struck. Television sets, some dead and
> most of the others crying out for intensive care, are
> scattered everywhere, along with packing crates and
> snaking piles of electronic debris. Paik, a short, roundish
> man with close-cropped black hair, pads in his slippers
> through the clutter, happily and completely at home.

Paik has discovered the artistic possibilities of television screens. Using them like the surface of a canvas, he creates abstract images with static and electronic "snow." The artist—whose work was honored in a 1982 retrospective at New York City's Whitney Museum—credits America's "playfulness and childish ideas" with his success. He tells why coming to the United States changed his career:

> America gave me access to high tech. Here I get a
> sense of what high-tech equipment can do to a sensibility.
> American kids have moved from "Sesame Street" to
> "The Electric Company" to MTV. They can see things
> in a screen that European kids can't.

Although Paik has gained recognition as an important artist, he belongs to an avant-garde world that remains unknown to most Americans, and his work does not directly reflect his Korean heritage. Americans seeking to understand Korean culture have often found it in the novels of Younghill Kang (1903–72), a writer and professor of comparative literature at New York University.

Kang's lyrical descriptions of his youth in occupied Korea appeared in his first novel, *The Grass Roof,* published in the United States in 1931:

In the 1930s Younghill Kang's memoirs of life in his homeland introduced American readers to the history and culture of Korea.

. . . in the mornings when the sun was getting up . . . its beams trembled on dew-shrunken foliage of the mountains, then poured down like sparkling bits of glass over the water in the valley—especially when the rice seeds were ripening in the fields. . . . In the spring, of course, this rice would be a clear young green, the color worn by brides in my country. But at all times the rice fields were . . . kept covered by water artificially, and mirrored the changes of the elements, reflecting the bright blue of the sky, taking on the colors of the slender rain, catching the dying sun in a blurred glass, and enhancing the mystery of the Yellow Dusk, or perhaps imaging the round moon above some scholar's roof.

Kang wrote his books in English, although he did not learn the language until he was 18 years old. After landing in San Francisco in the early 1920s, he traveled to New York City where he survived by working as a houseboy, waiter, dishwasher, and grocer while he attended school. According to his friend, author Bongyoun Choy, Kang first came to New York with only four dollars in his pocket. Nearing starvation, he walked into a Chinese restaurant and charmed the owner by writing a poem on the spot about vegetable soup. The restaurant then extended him a line of credit.

After several years in New York, Kang left to study literature, first in Canada and then at Harvard University. Upon returning to Manhattan, he launched his writing career, quickly attracting the attention of American literary eminences. In a 1931 review of *The Grass Roof*, the novelist Thomas Wolfe called Kang "a born writer . . . everywhere he is free and vigorous." By the 1950s Kang had firmly established his reputation. He then became involved in the politics of both the United States and Korea. A victim of Japan's occupation of Korea, he deplored oppression of any kind and fought against racism in the United States and against the dictatorial rule of South Korean president Syngman Rhee. Kang died at age 69 in 1972. His legacy not only gave Americans a window on the culture and history of Korea but also proved that Korean Americans could excel at art as well as science. ∾

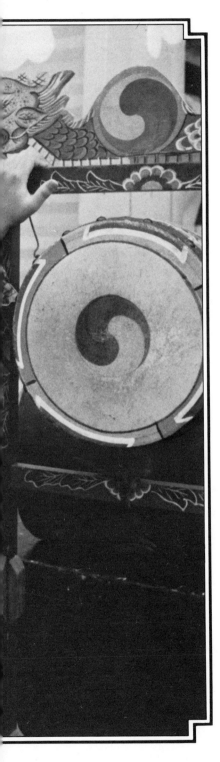

KOREAN AMERICANS AT HOME

While struggling to establish their businesses and to break into the professions, Koreans have also worked hard to understand and adjust to their daily lives in America. Immigrants often feel battered after a hard day of negotiating their way through streets, stores, and subway systems, trying simultaneously to make sense of both the English language and those who speak it.

Sometimes the strangeness of their new surroundings astonishes them, so dissimilar is life in America from that in Korea. One Korean-American woman still remembers her dismay when, as a graduate student in New York City, she saw a couple kissing in public. She ran to a professor for an explanation of this indecent behavior. "I was embarrassed, but it put my adviser in stitches," she said.

Koreans differ from Americans in their definition of proper behavior. Influenced by Confucian beliefs, they see morality as the fulfillment of a prescribed role in which parents and children, brothers and sisters, husbands and wives, all know what is expected of them and how they should act. Respect for elders is of such paramount importance that a child thinks nothing of sacrificing personal satisfaction in order to uphold filial

Social activist Grace Lyu Volckhausen has tried to better the lives of Korean-American women in New York.

duty. In contrast, second- and third-generation Americans—who generally hold sacred the idea of personal happiness—believe that the individual should strike out alone in search of success. This priority confounds Korean immigrants.

Women in the Workplace

As they adjust to being in the United States, Korean families are sometimes torn between Eastern and Western points of view. Women, in particular, have difficulty reconciling the traditional Confucian role of wife with that of an American working woman. In the old country, few ever worked outside the home, but once in the United States, almost 80 percent take paying jobs.

Many Korean-American women have continued the urban immigrant practice—begun in the 19th century—of toiling in poorly ventilated and sooty garment factories, popularly known as "sweatshops." Long the province of Jewish and Italian women, these unmarked loft buildings line the sidestreets of New York City's Seventh Avenue fashion district. A peek inside one of the 300 Korean-owned sweatshops reveals rows of women sitting amid the deafening clatter of their sewing machines, carefully guiding skirts, pants, and dresses under a rapid-fire needle.

Like their European predecessors of the early 20th century, Korean-American garment workers, who often spend 16-hour days in the shops, earn not an hourly wage but a flat rate for each piece of clothing they sew. This "piecework" system dates back to the beginnings of the garment industry and requires workers to speed through piles of clothing in order to make a decent wage.

Unlike most of their Jewish or Italian forebears, or their Central American co-workers, many Korean women in the factories have college degrees but do not speak enough English to find better-paying jobs. Garment work seems a natural choice because it requires no language skills; in addition, similar industries in Seoul (where many U.S. clothing manufacturers ship their material to be cut and sewn) employ females, a precedent followed by Korean shop owners in America.

A Community Advocate

Korean-American women often find themselves exhausted by grueling days such as those spent in garment factories, yet they continue to perform traditional wifely duties learned from their grandmothers and mothers: They frequently rise at dawn to prepare a Korean three-course breakfast, then go off to a job for another 12 to 16 hours. For a long time, despite being lonely for the companionship of female relatives at home and confused about the roles they were expected to play, Korean-American women remained stoical about their hardships. And because they appeared to be managing so well, nobody noticed their distress.

But one member of the Korean-American community, Grace Lyu Volckhausen, recognized that female immigrants needed help. In 1980 she began an outreach center at a YWCA in the borough of Queens, home to most of metropolitan New York City's Korean population. "I bridge a gap between cultures," Lyu Volckhausen told *Ms.* magazine. "But I don't tell these women what to do. It's not fair to do that. It's a matter of giving them endless information."

She realized that many Korean-American women are caught between the demands of two conflicting cultures. Their husbands depend on them to bring home extra income but also resent the new economic independence to which such responsibility leads: "In the first few years here, many men dream of going home to Korea so they can be the 'big cheese' again. But eventually they get used to it." Lyu Volckhausen's program offers counseling for such dilemmas and now boasts a membership of 1,000.

Conflicts between generations, Lyu Volckhausen says, can be as severe as those between husbands and wives. A Korean woman once telephoned her in tears to say that her teenage daughter had returned home from high school with a male classmate in order to work on a science project with him. The girl's grandmother had chased him out of the apartment with a broom. Lyu Volckhausen explains:

> It's a perfectly understandable event for a 70-year-old Korean grandmother who sees a 15-year-old grand-daughter with a 15-year-old boy in the same room. Confucius said that a woman and a man should not be in the same room after the age of seven. After I got the call from the mother crying hysterically, I got a call from the daughter crying hysterically. I told the girl, "You and your grandmother are both absolutely right. But how would you feel if you had just moved to, say, Timbuktu at the age of seventy?"

Generational Differences

Many Korean-American community centers provide day care for the children of working parents.

Many Korean-American households include an extended family of three generations, and they must deal with differences not only of age but also of values. Many

A little girl stands by as her mother sews garments in a New York City sweatshop.

grandparents and parents try to instill Old World customs in their children. A teenage girl described a typical conflict with her father: "Dad wants us to stand whenever he enters the room. We don't like it, and we make fun of him, but even though we don't take him seriously, we do it." Strict obedience to parents and grandparents is still the norm, one that Korean adolescents do not find among their American friends.

For their part, Korean-American parents are disgusted by the lack of respect American children show to their elders. One parent complains, "In America, kids don't get up and give their seats to the elderly on the bus. My kids see this and do the same thing." Disagreement can be particularly harsh between the child and the father because the latter—as the traditional head of the household—expects to decide his child's course of study, choice of college, profession, and even of spouse; arranged marriages are still the preferred method of finding a husband or wife.

Marriage and Friendship

Although they often view their parents' traditions as archaic, many Korean Americans in their twenties and thirties still perceive an arranged marriage as the "right way" to start their own families. A Korean American

Korean-American comedians Michael Young (left) and Steve Park burlesque the difficulties of learning to use a fork and knife.

who considers himself a cosmopolitan New Yorker explained why he preferred to let matchmaking relatives in Seoul find him a wife:

> My relatives back home knew when I would be coming to Korea and arranged meetings with four or five girls who came from good backgrounds. I chose one, we went out four or five times, and then got married. My friends here at the office could not understand how I could marry without knowing the girl. The truth is you can make a terrible marriage with someone you know three years. The chances are probably just as good for a bad marriage after three years of going together as after three months. It's after the marriage that you work together to build it, not before. I knew that my wife was Korean, that she came from a good family, and that she was very pretty. Of course I didn't love her when we got married—I hardly knew her. But we were ready to work at it and falling in love could come later.

Despite such rational thinking among Korean Americans, their divorce rate exceeds the national average. Arranged marriages will probably be among the first casualties of assimilation, much to the woe of the preceding immigrant generation. Many families are thrown into crisis as they try to guide their offspring and decide when American is "too" American. Parents and grandparents continually worry about children's abandoning traditional Korean culture and go to great expense each year to reinforce the younger generation's knowledge of their native land:

> I send my kids to Korea every year in the summertime and they learn about Korean heritage and culture, so they don't forget their parents' home country. That also means a good relationship with me because when they've grown up with an American-style education, they might eventually forget their parents. I would like to keep my son and daughter with me without any gaps in language or any gaps in anything.

Some families, however, see Americanization as an avenue to success and encourage their children to mingle with classmates. Even so, they voice hesitations about the younger generation's wholesale acceptance of new values.

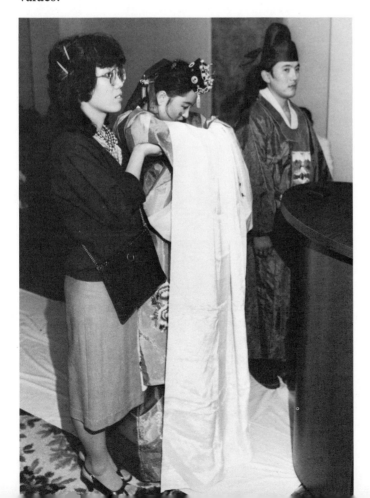

A Korean-American bride modestly hides her face during a traditional Buddhist marriage ceremony.

Korea's progress as an economic power and the recent influx of immigrants from the peninsula have sparked greater interest among Americans in Korean language and culture.

I'm not afraid of my kids' becoming too Americanized. I just want them to be ambitious and happy, and to see the world in a positive way. But there are two Korean traits that need to be retained. One is respect for elders. Here in the United States, I'm amazed to see elderly people deprived of anyone's attention. The other is that Koreans deal honestly. A handshake deal means more among Koreans. As an attorney, I see how little it means to Americans.

Frequent contact in school with non-Asians gives Korean-American teenagers the access to mainstream American society sometimes missed by their parents. The former are exposed to movies, television, and radio—conduits to popular culture and, more importantly, to the English language. Most grow up hearing Korean spoken at home but quickly gain proficiency in English by conversing with friends and studying in U.S. public schools.

Because older family members find it difficult to learn a new language, they use their native tongue almost exclusively. Families thus can be divided by a linguistic barrier; children try to communicate in English and are answered in Korean, a language that is becoming increasingly remote to them. Parents try to ease the problem of awkward communication by sending their children to special schools for weekly lessons in Korean. And although some adults avoid situations where they have to use English, most finally admit that they themselves need to be bilingual in order to get along in America.

In Pursuit of English

When Korean college graduates arrive in the United States, their inability to speak English drives many to work behind sewing machines, gas pumps, and produce counters despite years of experience in professional fields such as medicine, law, and banking. The director of an educational program for Asian immigrants calls English "the great prohibitor." Immigrants have found that using English not only opens new areas of employment to them but also wins them social acceptance. Koreans' willingness to communicate in English is especially important to residents of the traditionally ethnic neighborhoods where many immigrants settle. While Korean Americans generally bend over backward to get along with their non-Asian neighbors, their large numbers and evident success sometimes breed resentment. When tension between the two groups worsens, language can become the focus of controversy.

A Korean community group in the Philadelphia neighborhood of Olney recently tried to supplement existing English-language street signs with others written in Korean, explaining that elderly Koreans often became lost and confused. The city government had approved the suggestion but did not consult with the long-standing residents of the area. Incensed, Olney townspeople spray painted and defaced nearly all the Korean-language street signs. The issue of language had strained their acceptance of Korean immigrants to the breaking point.

Korean Churches

Since their earliest days in the United States, Koreans have traditionally sought support and understanding in Christian congregations. For new immigrants from the peninsula, churches traditionally have been both a refuge from the daily struggle to survive and a center for socializing, education, and political activism. The relationship between Koreans and American Christian missionaries dates back to the 19th century, when Methodist and Presbyterian teachers first convinced their Korean students they should go to the United States in order to get a Christian education. In addition, the influence of missionaries helped spur the immigration of the earliest group of Koreans that arrived in America, the Hawaiian plantation workers.

Although only 400 of the original 7,000 immigrants were Christian, those 400 soon set to work founding congregations in Hawaii. By 1918, 15 years after their

Controversy arose when Korean Americans introduced bilingual street signs to a Philadelphia neighborhood.

arrival on the islands, Koreans had established approximately 40 Protestant churches and had converted nearly 40 percent of their fellow plantation workers to Christianity.

The leaders of these churches performed a joint ministry of religion and social welfare, providing a spiritual home for poor, lonely, and illiterate plantation workers. After Sunday services, immigrants gathered to speak their native language, enjoy each other's company, and confide their problems. Whenever they met with adversity, Koreans turned to churches as a source of hope and solace.

As community centers, churches offered lessons in reading, history, and geography to their congregations. Church leaders never lost sight of their original mandate to bring education and democracy to Koreans, even though so many Koreans now lived in the West. Ministers founded evening schools where immigrants were trained to read and write their native tongue. By the 1920s illiteracy among newcomers belonged to the past.

As churches evolved into centers of community life, they expanded their functions. During the time of Japanese occupation of the peninsula, they became the headquarters for a movement of national liberation. Although the Japanese had forced Korea's puppet government to ban emigration, opponents of the invaders hoped to flee the country and organize a revolutionary army on foreign soil.

Some radicals escaped to Manchuria, in northern China. About 200 others slipped into the United States posing as students. This second category included many of those involved in church work. Unwilling to return to their homeland, where harsh reprisal probably awaited them, they rejected the menial labor available to them as Asians and committed themselves to establishing a U.S. base of resistance to the Japanese. The most famous of these radicals was Syngman Rhee, who in 1948 was elected the first president of South Korea.

The young patriots served as ministers and were supported by the American denominations they represented: Presbyterians, Methodists, Episcopalians, Baptists, and Roman Catholics. They opened church buildings to the needy, to the unemployed, and to students short of money. In the early 1900s a minister's salary ranged from $75 to $100 a month; many clergymen supplemented their incomes by running businesses such as laundries or grocery stores. Poor as they were, Korean ministers were known for their generosity and sometimes shared their own meager wages so their immigrant congregations wouldn't starve.

Serving the Community

Today, Korean-American churches continue to provide social services and to help immigrants find work and housing. In truth, many recent converts are attracted to Christianity for practical as well as spiritual reasons. Like the early Korean Christians in the West, they find support in neighborhood churches. After arriving in the United States, immigrants flock to a local priest or minister, hoping for guidance in a strange land. In the words of a social worker: "I've seen priests accompany Koreans to court, help them find jobs and counsel their families. They convert because the church provides these social functions." Thus, by accepting Protestantism and Catholicism, Koreans obtain a means of coping with their new lives. They also link themselves to a community center that introduces them to other Koreans and helps them preserve their heritage in the United States.

Today there are hundreds of Korean-American churches across the country, serving about 50 percent of that community. Half of all Korean-American Christians are Presbyterians, one quarter are Methodists, and the rest attend churches run variously by Lutherans, Roman Catholics, Episcopalians, Baptists, and the Assemblies of God. Many of those now arriving in America are drawn from South Korea's large Christian community (an estimated 30 percent of the total population), but even adherents of Buddhism—the country's most widespread faith—usually convert to Christianity when they reach U.S. shores.

Just as Koreans in America need the church, so the church needs Koreans. Sometimes after they have benefited from the aid of a minister or a particular program, immigrants are pressured to join congregations. Because many newcomers from South Korea move into dilapidated urban neighborhoods, they seem highly eligible replacements for worshipers who have fled from the city to the suburbs.

In New York City's borough of Queens, more than 300 Korean churches have sprung up during the past 10 years, and previously existing ones have tried to bolster small congregations by attracting immigrants. A 1986 article in the *New York Times* reported on the renaissance of a First United Methodist Church in the Queens neighborhood of Flushing.

Its membership had dropped to only 30 people, so the church's New York director decided to attract worshipers among the Koreans moving into the area. In 1976 they appointed a bilingual Korean pastor to lead the old congregation and also to begin a separate one for immigrants. Tensions sometimes ran high as the English- and Korean-speaking groups bickered about the use of space, the attention each received from the minister, the schedule of services, and the allotment of church funds.

Despite these problems, the church remained committed to its decision. The president of a New York City Presbyterian seminary commented on the new influx of immigrants into America's churches:

I admire congregations who are in the city and say, "These people are moving in and if that means changing the way we do things then we've got to do that." Mainline Protestant denominations have for the better part of their time in this country worked with a homogenous population: white and middle class or upper middle-class. It takes effort to accommodate diversity of worship styles, theological perspectives, cultural attitudes.

Choir members sing in their native tongue at a service held at the First United Methodist Church in Flushing, New York.

Korean-American ministers have been community leaders since the turn of the century.

Today, First United Methodist Church of Flushing has not one but three Korean ministers. All have adjusted their schedules to meet the demands—including house calls and nighttime appointments—of a congregation whose members often work 16-hour days. Each Sunday they help their Korean congregation find the strength it needs to continue a debilitating routine. One community member said, "Many Koreans want to expand their stores and they pray for that. They pray for family and health and pray for their children because Korean children are struggling in American schools when they first come here. The Korean parents pray that their children study well."

Traditionally, Korean Christians have an evangelical bent, and they tend to favor literal interpretations of the Bible. Bong-youn Choy, author of *Koreans in America*, writes, "Many ministers belong to orthodox . . . groups and emphasize disciplined Christian asceticism. Thus, they focus on personal faith in Christ and have little sensitivity to the social witness of the gospel."

Unlike the fiercely nationalistic Korean churches of the early 20th century, congregations today shy away from political activism and seem uninterested in such secular concerns as the unpopularity of the regime of President Chun Doo Hwan in Korea. Instead, they dedicate themselves to the well-being of their families, the success of their businesses, and the preservation of their inherited culture in the New World. Almost all observers of recent immigrants from the peninsula agree that religion and the church form the center of community life. One congregant from Flushing gives the Korean perspective on this phenomenon:

> Maybe living in another country makes us more devout.
> There are so many different standards that you can get
> attracted to, living in an entirely different situation,
> that your religion takes a very strong lead in your life.

THE STRUGGLE FOR DEMOCRACY

Although they have worked hard to establish themselves as an ethnic group distinct from all other Asians in the United States, Korean Americans tend to keep a low profile here. They typically focus their attention on private matters—work, family, and church life—eschewing involvement in the controversial realm of legal and political issues. Yet their seeming indifference to public affairs vanishes when unrest in their native country makes headlines around the world, as it did in the spring of 1987. Then, political passions surface, and Korean Americans demonstrate a strong attachment to the land and people of their ancestry.

The events of 1987, in particular, aroused Korean-American interest because they marked a new phase not only in the history of the peninsula's politics but also in the evolution of the long association between South Korea and the United States. In fact, the battle between the South Korean people and their government over such questions as honest elections and free speech dates back to the time when missionaries from the United States carried the ideals of democracy to Korea.

That legacy often seems to matter as little to the U.S. government as to the South Korean dictatorship.

In 1987 the U.S. ambassador to South Korea described the country's 1985 parliamentary elections as "free and fair," though most observers acknowledged that they had been rigged by the Chun government. The ambassador further admitted that the U.S. interest in Korea should be considered more important than that country's dreams of democracy.

This indifference galled South Koreans. They count on America to keep North Korea at bay and to understand that, in the words of one scholar, "Next to the Middle East, South Korea is probably the part of the world where American interests and world peace are most threatened." At the same time, America continues to support Chun, a president who would neither be elected nor tolerated in the United States.

Just as the U.S. government's attitude embittered them, so too did the memory of America's role in quelling a student-led protest in the city of Kwangju. It was there, in May 1980, that scores of civilians were killed by Korean soldiers from the Combined Forces Command, a unit of South Korean and American troops under U.S. authority, charged with guarding the sensitive zone separating North and South Korea.

The Kwangju killings touched a raw nerve among South Korean students and have come to symbolize all they resent about the United States: its authority; its indifference to South Korea's yearning for democracy; and its power to eliminate those who threaten the country's delicate stability. In 1987 the *New York Times* reported that when a university professor asked his class what the most important postwar event in the nation

In June 1987 a Korean woman hands flowers to Seoul police in full riot gear.

was, fully expecting them to say "the Korean War," almost all responded with one word: "Kwangju."

Recent Progress

Although opposition leaders to Chun's Democratic Justice party sometimes felt they must contend with two foes—the party itself and the U.S. administration that backs it—the movement made progress. Weeks of violent demonstrations in June 1987 resulted in a change in government policy, announced by the designated president, Roh Tae Woo. He relinquished his claim to the office and proposed that direct elections be held to choose the next president. This suggestion, made on national television, represented a major concession to protesters' demands and to the democratic process they fought for. Roh also said he wanted to restore the political rights of Kim Dae Jung, South Korea's most prominent opposition leader, who often had been held under house arrest by the current regime.

On June 12, 1987, Korean Americans gathered outside New York City's Korean Embassy to voice their support for South Korea's popular opposition leader, Kim Dae Jung.

As South Korea moved closer to holding free elections, its fate depended increasingly on the United States, a nation with the power to help—or hinder— the forces of democracy. The destinies of these countries became more intertwined, perhaps, than ever before: In the view of the United States, a stable South Korea decreased the chance of an invasion by North Korea, and thus would stave off a possibly catastrophic confrontation between America and the Soviet Union.

For this reason, in 1987 many South Koreans still believed that America would ultimately help them attain democratic rule. If, however, the United States continues to support an unpopular military regime, a crisis would result not only in South Korea but also among Korean Americans, whose confidence in their adopted homeland would be sorely tested. ❧

FURTHER READING

Choy, Bong-youn. *Koreans in America*. Chicago: Nelson-Hall, 1979.

Kang, Younghill, and Mirok Li. *The Grass Roof* and *The Yalu Flowers*. New York: W. W. Norton, 1975.

Kessner, Thomas, and Betty Boyd Caroli. *Today's Immigrants, Their Stories*. New York: Oxford University Press, 1982.

Kim, Ilsoo. *New Urban Immigrants, The Korean Community in New York*. Princeton, NJ: Princeton University Press, 1981.

Woo-Keun, Han. *The History of Korea*. Seoul, Korea: The Eul-Yoo Publishing Company, 1970.

INDEX

Picture credits

We would like to thank the following sources for providing photographs: AP/Wide World Photos: p. 37, 40, 43, 67, 73, 82, 96, 104; Asian Art Institute: pp. 52(top and & bottom), 53(top & bottom), 55; The Bettmann Archive: pp. 26, 48, 59; Bishop Museum, Honolulu, Hawaii: pp. 18–19, 45–46, 65; California Historical Society Library: p. 72; Mrs. Chung and the University of Hawaii's Women's Studies Program: p. 60; Denny Family Collection, Oregon Historical Society: p. 22; Freer Gallery of Art: p. 51(top); Hawaii State Archives: pp. 47, 61; Tom Kelly: p. 76; Korean Cultural Service: pp. 20, 50(top & bottom), 51(bottom); Corky Lee: pp. 12–13, 54(top), 68–69, 74, 86–87, 90, 91, 92, 100, 105; Library of Congress: pp. 16, 21, 27, 46; Yong Soon Min: p. 54(bottom); National Archives: p. 25; New York Public Library: pp. 62, 84; New York Times Pictures/Bruce Berman: p. 75; New York Times Pictures/Charles Higgins: p. 99; Oregon Historical Society: p. 64; Ken Regan Camera 5: p. 49; Reuters/Bettmann Newsphotos: pp. 39, 102–103; John Schultz, PAR/NYC: p. 14; Katrina Thomas: p. 93; United Nations: pp. 35, 38; UPI/Bettmann Newsphotos: p. 17, 28, 29, 30, 31, 32, 36, 71, 79, 80–81; *U.S. News & World Report*: p. 56; Visual Communications, Southern California Asian American Studies Central Inc.: p. 94; Grace Lyu Volckhausen: p. 88

BRIAN LEHRER is a free-lance journalist in New York City whose work includes the award-winning radio documentary "Immigrant New York: The Last Twenty Years." He contributes articles to many magazines, reports for NBC Radio, and teaches at the Columbia University Graduate School of Journalism.

DANIEL PATRICK MOYNIHAN is the senior United States senator from New York. He is also the only person in American history to serve in the cabinets or subcabinets of four successive presidents—Kennedy, Johnson, Nixon, and Ford. Formerly a professor of government at Harvard University, he has written and edited many books, including *Beyond the Melting Pot, Ethnicity: Theory and Experience* (both with Nathan Glazer), *Loyalties*, and *Family and Nation*.